SCHOLASTIC BOOK OF Hindu Gods and Goddesses

Retold By Deepa Agarwal

Illustrated By Rayika Sen

SCHOLASTIC

New York Toronto London Auckland

Sydney New Delhi Hong Kong

Contents

Too Many Modaks for Ganesha!

It was the time of the year Ganesha awaited eagerly. The time of the puja was special to him—Ganesh Chaturthi. People who loved Ganesha made idols of the god. They set them up in their houses and worshipped them. And what did they offer to their beloved Ganesha? His favourite sweet, modak.

Ganesha loved modaks. And he could not bear to disappoint anyone who worshipped him. So he sat on Mushika's back and visited each and every house that had set up his idol. (In case you don't know, Mushika is the mouse that carries Ganesha around.) In each house Ganesha ate some modaks. But he ate too many. There was not enough space for them in his tummy.

So they began to push and shove each other inside him. They jabbed and jostled so hard that Ganesha's tummy began to feel wriggly and squirmy. It was not a good feeling at all.

'Ohhh ... arggh!' Ganesha began to groan. 'Ohhhh ... arghh! Ouch! These modaks ... ohhh! What am I to do?'

Then he got an idea. Maybe I should go outside, he thought. The cool night air might calm these wriggly modaks down.

So he called Mushika and said, 'Come on, friend, take me for a round of the city.'

'Another round? Are you planning to eat more modaks?' Mushika's eyes almost popped out.

'Don't be silly!' Ganesha said. 'I just need some fresh air. These modaks are wriggling too much in my tummy. It might calm them down.'

Ganesha sat on Mushika's back and set off. It was a lovely night. The moon, Chandradev, was shining extra bright, and the air was cool and fresh.

'Ahh ... I'm already beginning to feel better,' Ganesha said, letting out a big burp.

But just then Mushika let out a loud squeak. He jumped high up into the air. So high that Ganesha tumbled off. Thump! He fell on the ground. And when he fell, something happened. The modaks in his tummy decided to escape. They pushed as hard as they could. So hard that Ganesha's tummy split open.

All the modaks rolled out.

'My modaks! My yummy modaks have fallen out!' Ganesha cried. 'Why did you jump like that, you silly Mushika?'

'B-b-but th-there is a snake!' Mushika's teeth chattered. 'It came out so suddenly! I was afraid th-that it might bite me.'

'A snake? Hmm ...' Ganesha saw a snake wriggling away. It looked very pleased with itself. He grabbed hold of the snake. 'You frightened Mushika,' he scolded. 'You made my modaks fall out. Now you'd better make up for it.'

Ganesha reached out with his trunk and quickly shoved all the modaks back into his tummy.

'I can't waste such yummy modaks,' he said. 'My tummy has a big slit. But you will make a nice belt to hold it together, snake.' He tied the snake tightly around his belly. 'Now my modaks will be safe,' he said.

Just as he had tucked in the last modak, he heard a loud laugh. 'Who's laughing?' Ganesha cried, offended.

'Ha ha ha! What a funny sight you make! Ha ha ha!'

Someone laughed again. 'You've made me laugh so much that I'm afraid my tummy might split open too. But there aren't any modaks inside it! Ha ha ha! I must share this joke with my twenty seven wives.'

It was Chandradev, the moon. 'How dare you make fun of me!' Ganesha yelled. He felt so angry that he wanted to throw something at the moon. But there was nothing to throw. Not a single stick or stone in sight.

Ganesha was so angry that he broke off one of his tusks. He threw the broken-off piece at the moon with all his strength.

'I'll see how you laugh now!' Ganesha yelled.

The tusk flew through the air, up into the sky, and hit the moon very hard. Crash! Bang! So hard that the moon's bright round face broke into two pieces.

'You know that I'm the god who blesses people with good luck. I remove all their difficulties,' Ganesha went on. 'Since you laughed at me, from today you will bring bad luck on people. Anyone who looks at you will have bad luck.'

Ganesha calmed down after he had taught the moon a lesson. But a terrible thing happened when Chandradev was broken into two halves. Moonlight disappeared from the earth. The night became pitch dark.

The people of the city began to cry out in fear. 'What has happened? Why has it become so dark? Has a demon eaten up the moon on this holy day of Ganesh Chaturthi?'

Even the gods became worried. 'I am sorry, I am sorry!' Ganesha heard a voice crying from the sky.

‘Please take back your curse. I’ll never make fun of you again. Please, I don’t want to bring bad luck on people.’

Ganesha did not know what to do now. He had not meant to break the moon into two. He had just wanted to stop Chandradev from laughing at him. He was beginning to feel sorry that the light of the moon had vanished and people were afraid of the dark.

‘Do something,’ Mushika squeaked. ‘He should not have laughed at you. But we need moonlight to see at night.’

Ganesha shook his head. ‘Once a curse has left your mouth, you cannot undo it,’ he said sadly. ‘It’s not like modaks.’

‘But can’t you add something that makes it milder?’ Mushika asked. ‘What will happen to the earth if the moon cannot shine?’

'Yes, Ganesha, make your curse milder!' The gods called from the heavens. They were extremely worried.

Ganesha thought for a while. How was he to solve this terrible problem? 'Alright, I cannot take back my curse,' he said to the moon, finally. 'But I can put you together again. I can also take away most of the bad luck.'

'Oh please do that! I'll never laugh at you again, I promise!' the moon cried.

'I can't make you completely whole again,' Ganesha said. 'But I can do one thing. For fifteen days you will grow in size and on the fifteenth day you will be whole again. People will call that the full moon day. Then for fifteen days you will grow smaller, and on the fifteenth day you will be as fine as an eyelash.

'People will call that the new moon day. And on this day, Ganesh Chaturthi, the day you laughed at me, anyone who looks at you will be cursed with bad luck.'

'Thank you, Ganeshji,' said the moon softly. 'You have saved me.'

The moon began to glow again, but not so brightly. A big black scar had appeared on its bright face where Ganesha's tusk hit it. But on the first day of the month it was whole again and shone in all its glory.

So, this is the story people tell, that ever since Ganesha cursed it, the moon keeps changing in size. It grows bigger and bigger for fifteen days till it becomes full. Then it becomes smaller and smaller till it almost disappears.

And people still believe that it is unlucky to look at the moon on Ganesh Chaturthi.

How Ganesha Wrote the Mahabharata

The great sage Ved Vyas sat outside his hut, thinking very hard. He was a very learned man. He had divided the Hindu holy book, *The Vedas*, into four parts. He did it because he felt it would be easier for people to understand it that way. That is why he had been named Ved Vyas—the man who divided *The Vedas*.

Right now, however, a different idea had come into Ved Vyas's head. The idea of a great story that had almost everything possible in it. It was a story about gods and saints and ordinary women and men. It was about fathers and mothers, brothers and sisters, uncles, aunts and cousins, friends and enemies. It was about good deeds and evil deeds. Some of the people in this story were helpful and kind but others were cruel and wicked. Some risked their lives to help others but others tried to cheat or kill them. And some people were partly good and partly bad. In other words, it was a story about real life.

'All the people in the world need to know this story,' he thought. 'It will help them in many ways.

They will learn that it is better to be kind than cruel. They will learn that the most important thing is to do your duty. They will also learn that you should work hard sincerely without thinking of rewards.

'But how am I to spread this story through the world? It is a very long story. If I start writing it, I might forget some parts. I need someone else to write down this story while I keep making it up. It will have to be someone very quick and with good handwriting. How am I going to find such a person?'

Ved Vyas thought and thought for a long time. Then he got an idea. 'Maybe Brahma, the creator, who made this universe, can help me,' he thought. So he closed his eyes and began to pray to Brahma.

He prayed very hard and long.

Ved Vyas prayed so long and hard that finally his prayer reached Brahma.

'It looks like the learned Ved Vyas has a problem,' Brahma said. 'I must go to his help. Immediately he flew to Ved Vyas's hut. 'What is your problem, learned sage?' he asked. 'Why were you trying to reach me?'

Ved Vyas was overjoyed to see Brahma. He bowed low before Brahma and said, 'Respected Lord Brahma, I need your advice. I have thought of a great story, one that will help all the people on the earth. It is complete in my mind. But it is very long. I'm afraid I'll miss out some important parts if I try to write it myself. I need someone to write it down while I narrate it.'

'You say it is a very long story. There is only one person who can do this job,' Brahma said. 'The elephant-headed god, Ganesha, who has the power to remove problems. Ask him. He will be the right person to write such a long story.'

Ved Vyas began to pray to Ganesha now. And after some time Ganesha arrived at his hut.

'Greetings, Lord Ganesha,' Ved Vyas said, folding his hands and bowing. 'Thank you so much for answering my prayer.'

'What can I do for you, respected Ved Vyas?' Ganesha replied. 'Why does a learned sage like you need my help?'

'Lord Ganesha, you have the power to solve all problems. Whenever people begin a new task, they pray to you so that they may complete it without any difficulty,' Ved Vyas said. 'I'm beginning a new and very important task and need your blessings. But I need something more from you as well.'

'I am more than happy to give you my blessings for this important task, learned sage,' Ganesha said. 'What else can I do for you?'

'I have thought of a great story,' Ved Vyas replied. 'One that will help all the people on the earth. It is complete in my mind. But it is very long. I'm afraid I'll miss out some important parts if I try to write it myself. I need someone to write it down while I narrate the story. Please, will you write this story for me?'

'You are one of our most learned sages. I am sure this story will be of great value to the people of the earth. How can I refuse to be part of this great work?' Ganesha asked. 'But you say it is a very long story. That means it will take a long time to write. I will write it on one condition. You must not stop at all while you are telling me the story. If you do, I will stop too.'

Ved Vyas frowned. It would be very difficult to tell such a long story without stopping at all. Then he got an idea. 'Agreed,' he said. 'But I too have a condition. You must understand the meaning of each and every sentence that I recite.'

'Agreed,' Ganesha said with a smile.

Ved Vyas sent for a huge stack of birch bark sheets and a feather pen and ink for Ganesha to write with.

'Sri Ganesha!' he said, with a bow to Ganesha. 'So begins my story ... A long long time ago ...'

The story poured from Ved Vyas's mouth like a rushing river. Ganesha's feather pen began to move across the birch bark at equal speed too.

It was a very long story, as Ved Vyas had said. He narrated it in verses known as shlokas. Days and nights passed and shlokas continued to pour from his mouth. And Ganesha continued to write, not stopping for a second. In between, just for fun, Ved Vyas would make up long and difficult shlokas. Ganesha would have to stop to think about their meaning. This gave Ved Vyas a chance to rest a bit.

And then, something terrible happened. While he was writing, Ganesha's quill or pen broke into two.

'My pen!' Ganesha cried. 'My pen broke. I need another pen quickly. I can't stop!' He looked around, worried. But there was no other pen nearby.

'I can't stop!' Ganesha cried again. 'I need a pen right away!' Then he got an idea. Quickly he broke off one of his tusks. He dipped it in ink and continued to write as fast as ever. In this way, Ganesha continued to write the story till Vyas reached the end.

It is said that it took three years to write down this great story. Ved Vyas named it "Jaya" or "Victory" because it was about a war between two groups of cousins, the Kauravas and the Pandavas. We know it as *The Mahabharata*. It is a very long story. There are more than a hundred thousand shlokas in *The Mahabharata*.

As time passed, this story spread through the whole of India and later around the whole world. And all who have heard it or read it agree it is one of the greatest stories of all time.

How Indra Got his Vajra

The gods were extremely worried. As they watched from the heavens, they noticed that the people of the earth were roaming everywhere, searching for water. Children were crying with thirst, old people were falling down on dry and dusty pathways begging for a sip of water.

The leaves on the branches of trees and bushes had withered. The grass had shrivelled. The crops lay shrunken in the fields.

'Something has to be done,' said Brahma, 'or all mankind will perish.'

'The green and fertile Earth had turned into a wasteland,' said Vishnu. 'It is the work of that asura, that evil demon Vritra. He's taken the form of a dragon and has swallowed up all the water in the world to show his power.'

'Indra will have to destroy him,' said Shiva. 'He is the one responsible for his birth.'

Vritra had been created by Tvashta, one of the creator gods, to take revenge on Indra for the death of his three-headed son Trishiras. Tvashta had performed a powerful ritual and this fearful asura had emerged from the sacrificial fire.

'I have made you so strong that no weapon created till now can destroy you,' said Tvashta to Vritra. 'Go and slay Indra. Avenge your brother's murder.'

The demon let out a terrible laugh. 'With pleasure,' he said.

Tvashta set off to find Indra. As he approached the heavens, his body began to grow. It grew so large that it appeared he would cover the whole universe. A fearful glow came from him, blinding anyone close by. His hair was the colour of melted copper, and so were his moustache and beard.

When he let out his war cry and shook his trident, all the three worlds trembled as if Vritra had set off an earthquake. Then he yawned, opening his huge dragon mouth which looked large enough to swallow the earth and the sky. And in one gulp he drank up all the water on the earth.

After that Vritra attacked the gods with a powerful army of asuras and drove Indra from his throne.

Indra fled to save his life and hurried to ask Vishnu for help. 'There is only one way out,' Vishnu said gravely. 'We have to create the most

powerful weapon ever, to kill this dreadful asura.'

'Please do that, Lord Vishnu,' Indra begged.

'It is not so simple,' Vishnu said with a worried frown. 'We will need Rishi Dadhichi's help. Let us go to his ashram right away.'

The gods hurried to Dadhichi's hermitage. Years ago, the gods had defeated the asuras in a terrible battle. After that they had left their divine weapons with the sage to keep them safe.

The gods were worried that the demons might perform some magic that would make their weapons useless. But they felt that the asuras

would never try to steal their weapons from Dadhichi since all his prayers and fasts had made the sage very powerful.

For many years the weapons lay with Dadhichi. Then he got tired of guarding them. Using a special mantra, he dissolved them in holy water and drank it up.

The gods arrived at Dadhichi's ashram and after greeting the sage respectfully, they asked for their weapons.

But the sage said, 'You did not come for so many years. I decided to dissolve them in water and drink it up. Now the power of your weapons has gone into my bones.'

The gods looked at each other, full of dismay. Finally Indra said, 'Most holy sage, a terrible demon named Vritra is about to destroy all creation. No weapon that we possess is strong enough to kill him. What should we do?'

The sage thought for a while, then he said, 'You will have to create an undefeatable weapon. A weapon with the power of thunder. That can only be made out of my bones. They are so strong now that nothing can break them.'

'What are you saying, holy one!' Vishnu exclaimed. 'How can we ask you to sacrifice your life to kill Vritra?'

'Someone has to make the sacrifice to save the universe from this evil creature,' Dadhichi replied calmly. 'When I pass away, make a weapon called the vajra from my bones. It will not fail against Vritra.'

Dadhichi began to meditate. After a while a fiery glow began to appear from his chest. Even as the gods watched, his body melted away and only his bones were left. The gods bowed to the ground in gratitude.

'Dadhichi's great sacrifice must never be forgotten,' Vishnu said. He picked up the bones and fashioned a weapon out of them. 'This is the vajra, the most deadly thunderbolt,' he said, handing it to Indra. 'Use it well, O Indra. Go and save the universe from destruction.'

Indra folded his hands to all the gods. 'Bless me, O devas,' he said humbly.

All the gods showered their blessings upon Indra. Then he picked up the vajra and set off for Vritra's stronghold.

Vritra had created a hundred fortresses around him. Using his magic powers he had made them so strong that it was impossible to break in.

He was living in the innermost one, feasting and enjoying life.

'Did you see how the gods fled?' he was bragging to his demon followers that day.

The asuras laughed. 'They are cowards,' one said. 'Now the universe is ours.'

'Yes, only ours, and I am all powerful!' Vritra yelled as he shook his huge mace.

Just then a loud booming sound made them jump. 'What's that?' Vritra cried. 'Who made that sound?'

The sound came again and again. Little did Vritra know that with the help of the vajra, Indra was razing each of the ninety nine fortresses to the ground, one by one.

'It's just some rocks rolling around,' said the demons. 'What else could it be?' They continued their feasting.

Then, some of Vritra's guards came running into the banquet hall.

'Why are you bothering me?' Vritra yelled at them, annoyed. 'Can't you see we are eating?'

'Your majesty, the impossible has happened!' they cried, shaking with terror. 'Indra is attacking us. He has destroyed almost all the fortresses!'

'Indra!' Vritra grabbed his mace. 'How dare he disturb me! I'll settle him once and for all!'

The asura charged out to defend his fortress. A terrible battle began. Vritra turned into a dragon again and blew deadly flames and smoke from his mouth at Indra. And he lashed him with his spiky tail.

But Indra had the vajra to protect him. In the end, none of the asura's weapons were strong enough. Indra killed him with a mighty clap of thunder. Then he slashed the dragon's belly open and released the waters Vritra had captured.

The waters flowed back into the thirsty world. Overjoyed and relieved, people rushed to the refilled ponds and rivers and drank thirstily from them. So did all the animals. The grass began to grow again, the crops revived and leaves sprouted on trees.

The gods returned to the heavens and all was well again. Ever since then, the vajra or thunderbolt has remained Indra's special weapon.

Is the Sun a Mango?

Hanuman was the son of Anjana and the wind god Vayu. Anjana used to be an apsara at Indra's court and her original name was Punijkastala. Once she made fun of a meditating monkey sage and playfully threw rocks at him. His meditation was disturbed, and he was very hurt that she was making fun of him. He cursed her to be reborn as a vanar or monkey. When Punijkastala begged for mercy, the sage said that once she gave birth to a son she would be freed from the curse.

Punijkastala turned into a monkey named Anjana. She got married to Kesari, the king of the monkeys or vanars. Many years passed but they had no children. This made both of them very sad. Anjana, however, did not give up. She continued to pray to Shiva and Parvati to bless her with a child.

King Dashrath of Ayodhya too had no children. A priest advised him to perform a special puja. Kheer was to be given to all the king's wives as prasad. This prasad would act as a blessing for the wives and soon they would give birth to the children they were longing for.

Vayu, the wind god, was passing by. He knew that Anjana had been praying long and hard for a child.

He swept away some of the blessed kheer and

blew it into Anjana's mouth. Soon she became pregnant and in the course of time gave birth to a lovely child. Because Vayu had brought the blessed kheer, Hanuman came to be known as the son of Vayu. The god passed on many of his qualities to him too.

Little Hanuman was very playful and mischievous. One day, he woke up feeling very hungry. He wanted to ask his mother for something to eat. But he couldn't find her anywhere.

'Ma! Ma! Where are you?' he called.

His mother did not reply to his call. Surprised, Hanuman stepped outside and looked all around for his mother. He glanced up at the sky and his

eye fell on the sun. Hanuman stared at it. He had never seen the sun. What was this thing hanging in the sky?

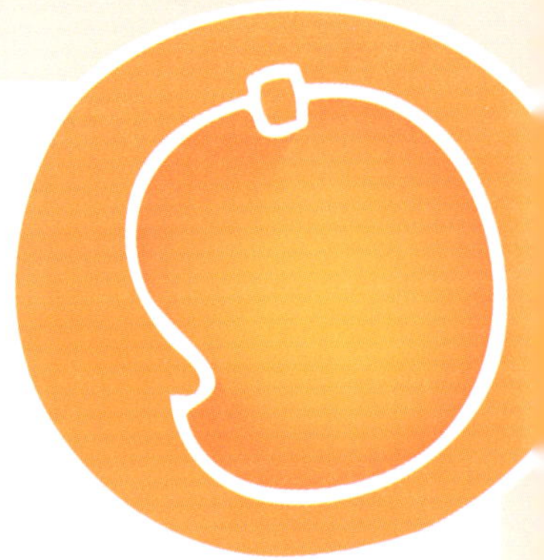

He wondered. It was round and bright orange in colour. It had to be a ripe mango.

Hanuman's mouth began to water. He wanted to suck on a juicy mango. It was high up in the sky but that was no problem for the son of Vayu, the wind.

He could soar through the skies easily. Immediately Hanuman zoomed into the air.

Little Hanuman did not know that someone else was heading towards the sun too. It was the mighty demon Rahu. Every now and again Rahu caused eclipses by swallowing the sun. It was time for an eclipse right then.

As luck would have it, both of them reached the sun at the same time.

'Where have you appeared from, little monkey?' Rahu called. 'Get out of my way. I'm going to eat the sun.'

'No! I'm going to eat it!' Hanuman cried.

'How dare you challenge me, little monkey! Don't you know who I am?' Rahu yelled angrily. 'I'm the mighty Rahu and I'm supposed to eat the sun!'

'But I'm really hungry. I am going to eat this juicy mango, so you get out of the way!' Hanuman replied.

Rahu tried to frighten Hanuman with his big teeth but Hanuman just laughed. 'Alright, if you're not going to listen, you will have to learn the hard way!' Rahu growled. He reached out with his long arms and tried to push Hanuman out of the way. He pushed and pushed. But he could not move Hanuman from his place by even an inch.

The mighty Rahu was really furious now. He began hitting and kicking Hanuman with all his strength. But the child god did not cry out once. Rahu's furious blows had no effect on him. He did not allow Rahu to get close to the sun. In fact, he

beat Rahu back with such force that the demon was terrified.

Rahu's defeat made him very angry. At once he flew to Indra, the king of the gods, to complain.

Indra was reclining on his throne, watching his apsaras dance. He was surprised to see Rahu flying to him in a tizzy.

'What are you doing here, Rahu?' he asked. 'I thought you had to swallow the sun at this time and cause an eclipse.'

'Your majesty,' Rahu cried, 'an unheard-of thing has happened. As I approached the sun, a monkey child came in the way. He said that he wanted to eat the sun and would not move when I told him to. Worse still, he's so strong that I could not push him aside.'

'A child? A monkey's child? How dare he?' Indra was in a rage. 'I will fix him.'

Hanuman was just about to swallow the sun when he received a terrible blow. The furious Indra had thrown his vajra or thunderbolt at him. It struck Hanuman hard on his jaw. Immediately he fell to the earth and became unconscious. Worse, the vajra left a permanent mark on his chin. This is how the monkey god got the name Hanuman. *Hanuh* means jaw in Sanskrit.

His mother Anjana had been looking for him everywhere. When he fell to the ground, badly hurt, she was horrified. She wept bitterly to see her little son lying there unconscious. When she asked around, she came to know the whole story.

Anjana hurried to complain to Hanuman's father, Vayu. 'Is it right that the king of the gods should use such force against a mere child?' she sobbed. 'The boy could have lost his life. How could an innocent child know about the eclipse? Rahu could have explained it gently to him and Indra could have been more understanding.'

Vayu shook with rage when he heard what had happened. 'Indra dared to hurt our child! He thinks he is the most powerful among the gods. He does whatever he pleases !' he said. 'I'll teach him a lesson he won't forget in a hurry. No one will dare ill-treat our son again.'

To punish Indra, Vayu decided to take away all air from the earth. The result was that all living beings began to choke to death. Their gasps and cries reached the heavens.

'Vayu is angry; he has taken away air from the earth!' The news spread everywhere.

'Why?'

'Because Indra hurt his little son.'

The gods rushed to Indra's palace. 'Lord Indra, do something soon, or all living beings will die!'

Indra had no choice now but to take away the effect of his thunderbolt. All the gods gathered around the unconscious Hanuman to help revive him. To appease Vayu, they blessed him with many boons.

Brahma gave Hanuman a boon that would protect him from any weapon in war. It would also create fear in his enemies and destroy fear in his friends. He granted Hanuman the ability to change his form at will and to travel wherever he wished with ease.

Shiva blessed him with the gift of a long life. He granted him knowledge of the scriptures, as well as the ability to cross the ocean easily.

Indra also gave his blessings, saying that Hanuman's body would become stronger than even the vajra. He would be immune to it now.

Varun, the god of the sea, declared that Hanuman would always be safe in water. Agni blessed him with immunity from fire. Surya, the sun god, gave him two powers—"laghima" and "garima". This was the ability to become as small or as large as he wished.

Yama, the god of death, blessed him with a healthy life. He even freed Hanuman from his weapon, danda, so death would not come to him. Kuber, the god of wealth, declared that Hanuman would always remain happy and contented.

Vishwakarma granted the boon that Hanuman would be safe from all the objects or weapons he created.

Finally, his father Vayu blessed him with more speed than he himself had. And now that his son had been made so strong, he restored air to the earth.

Young Hanuman was thus transformed into an immensely powerful being. He always used his strength to help others and destroy evil.

Ram's Bridge

Ram stood on the shore of the sea and watched the waves sadly. The island of Lanka was not very far away—only the sea lay in between. But Ram had to cross the sea to reach Lanka. It was easier said than done.

It had taken him months to reach this place, Rameshwaram, and he was desperate to reach Lanka. His beloved wife Sita was imprisoned there and he had to rescue her somehow.

Ravan, the ten-headed demon king of Lanka, had carried her away using magic to trick Ram and his brother Lakshman and the kind-hearted Sita herself. Faithful Jatayu had tried to save her, but Ravan had wounded him mortally with his sword. Still Jatayu stayed alive long enough to tell Ram what had happened.

Ram and Lakshman had immediately hurried through the dense forests towards Lanka. On the way they had come to the kingdom of Kishkindha where they met Hanuman and his fellow vanars. After they helped the vanar king Sugreev regain his kingdom, he sent a band of his people to help them.

Hanuman used his divine powers to find out where exactly Sita was imprisoned in Lanka, and they headed there with all speed.

But now they had reached the ocean that separated Lanka from Bharat and were faced with a serious problem. How were they to cross the ocean?

Ram decided to pray to Samudra, the god of the ocean, to help him. If he worshipped Samudra with heart and soul, he thought, the god might part the sea for him. He fasted and prayed for three days and three nights. But the ocean god remained silent. He did not utter a word to respond to Ram's appeal.

This made Ram very angry. On the fourth day he stood up from his worship and called out to the god, 'Samudra! Samudra! Why don't you answer my prayers?'

Samudra still did not reply. This made Ram angrier still. He shot arrow after arrow into the sea. The arrows pierced many of the innocent creatures of the sea and they began to die. Lakshman, Hanuman and the vanars watched horrified.

'What are you doing, my brother?' Lakshman cried. 'These beings have not harmed you!'

'If the lord of the ocean does not want to answer my prayers, I have no choice but to destroy it and its inhabitants,' Ram shouted in a rage. 'Now I will shoot my brahmastra at the waves. Its power will make them dry up and a path will be carved through the ocean for my army.'

The brahmastra was a fearful weapon, capable of destroying all creation.

'Please think again, dear brother,' Lakshman begged. 'Calm down. You know how dangerous the brahmastra can be.'

'How can you ask me to calm down, Lakshman?' Ram cried. 'I can think of nothing but my poor Sita's suffering. I prayed to Samudra most devotedly, made all the required offerings and he still refuses to help. I have every right to destroy the ocean.'

Lakshman had no reply to this. He too wished to rescue Sita as soon as they could.

Just as Ram prepared to shoot the brahmastra, Samudra rose from the sea with folded hands.

'Forgive me, Ram,' he said. 'Please don't dry up the sea. So many beings will die. I will calm the waves so you can pass through without any problem. But you will have to build a bridge first. Fortunately, you have Nala, the son of Vishwakarma, in your vanar sena. Ask him to direct the other monkeys.'

Nala stepped forward. 'Yes! Indeed I'm the son of Vishwakarma, the architect of the gods,' he said. 'But why are you acting so proud, Samudra? Ram asked you for help with great love and humility. You answered only when he threatened you. This behaviour does not suit a god like you.'

After he showed his anger to Samudra, Nala turned to Hanuman. 'Let us begin work,' he said briskly. 'We will need many logs and rocks for the bridge.'

'Luckily, there are enough of us to finish the work very soon,' Hanuman said. 'Come on, brothers, let us start building the bridge.'

Nala called his brother Neel to help him, and the two supervised the building of the bridge. The vanar sena got to work, felling trees and gathering boulders. They picked up huge rocks as large as mountains and hurled them into the sea.

But it did not turn out to be a smooth task. 'They are sinking! They are sinking!' the vanars cried out in dismay, when they put the rocks in the water.

'I will see to it that they stay afloat,' Samudra immediately promised.

The rocks did not sink after that but another problem arose. They would not stick together to form a bridge, and began to float off in different directions.

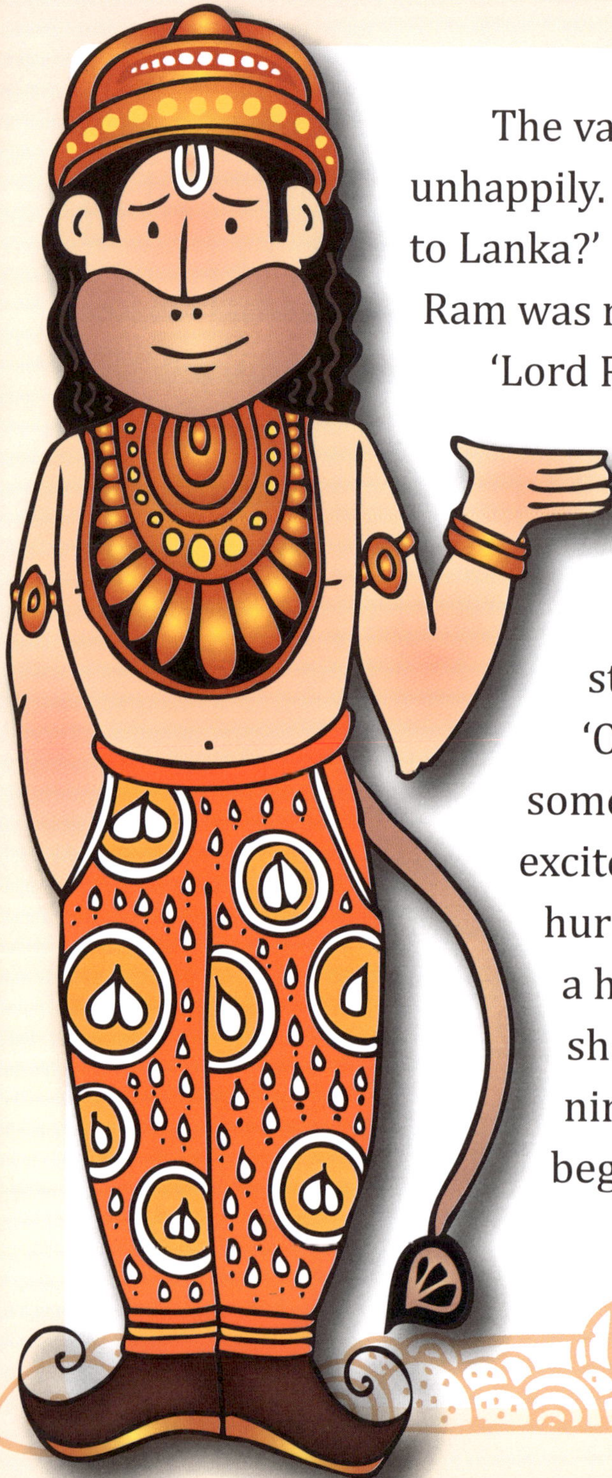

The vanar sena watched unhappily. 'Will we ever get to Lanka?'

Ram was ready to tear his hair.

'Lord Ram,' Hanuman said with folded hands. 'I think that if we write your name on the rocks, they will stay together.'

'Oh ... I think I forget something in all the excitement!' Nala said, hurriedly jumping over a huge boulder. 'We should worship the first nine stones for a good beginning. They would act as the symbols of the gods of the nine planets.' He beckoned his fellow monkeys to bring nine stones quickly.

Ram worshipped the stones and wrote his name on them. After that the bridge grew like magic and was completed in five days.

Ram took the first step on it, then Lakshman, followed by Hanuman. The army of monkeys and bears scampered after them happily and they all reached Lanka.

Ram
Ram
Ram
Ram

How Ganga Came to the Earth

The mighty King Sagar of the Sun dynasty ruled Ayodhya. He had won many battles and become very powerful. This king was also blessed with 60,000 sons, born to his wife Sumati. It was an extraordinary number of children for anyone to have. For this reason people said that he had got these sons through his magic powers.

Sumati had given birth to a gourd which burst open, and 60,000 babies came out. They were kept in jars of ghee and tended by faithful nurses.

King Sagar now wanted to show that there was no other ruler as powerful as him in the whole earth. So he decided to perform the great horse sacrifice or Ashvamedha yajna. This sacrifice was performed by kings when they wanted to prove there was no one as great as them.

Sagar gave instructions to bring the finest horse in his stables.

'Let this horse loose to gallop through all the territories nearby,' he commanded. 'And let my army of sons go with it. Whichever area the horse races through will be considered a part of my kingdom. If anyone stops the horse, my army will battle it out with them.'

Sagar's horse sped through the earth. The king's 60,000 sons accompanied it. When people heard it was King Sagar's horse and saw his huge army of sons behind it, everyone stepped aside. No one dared to stop it.

Soon Indra, the king of the gods, got the news that King Sagar's horse and army of sons was travelling over the earth claiming it for the king. And no one had dared to challenge them.

'This Sagar has become too strong for my good,' Indra thought. 'Today he is claiming the earth, tomorrow he will claim my throne. I must do something about this.'

Indra came down to the earth to see for himself. Then, using his divine powers, he stole the horse at night. But where was he to keep it? As he wandered through the forest with the horse, Indra reached the ashram of the sage Kapila.

The sage was in such deep meditation that he did not notice the god's arrival.

'This is the perfect place to hide the horse,' Indra thought. 'Let's see what this proud king does now.'

Indra flew back to heaven. When they discovered that the chosen horse was missing, Sagar's 60,000 sons got very angry. Immediately they set out to search for it. Full of rage, they went on a rampage, killing people and burning their houses. Finally they arrived at Rishi Kapila's ashram. They found the sage deep in meditation and the horse tied to a tree near him.

'This unholy sage spirited away our horse!' one of the princes cried.

'Let us teach him a lesson!' shouted the others. 'He is pretending to meditate. Let us end his meditation.'

'Yes, let's light a fire under him,' said one.

'Good idea!' laughed the others.

And they set the place where the sage was sitting on fire.

When the sage felt the heat of the fire, he opened his eyes. At the sight of the flames and the mocking faces of the princes, he flew into a rage.

'Wicked boys, now you shall feel the heat of my rage!' he cried. Burning sparks flew from his eyes and immediately reduced the 60,000 princes to ashes.

The terrible news spread fast and reached King Sagar.

'All my sons! All dead!' He wept bitterly. His queens, courtiers and the whole city was plunged into the deepest grief.

King Sagar's sons had perished, but their last rites had to be performed for the salvation of their souls. So the king sent his grandson Anshuman to apologise to the sage and get the ashes and the horse back.

Anshuman approached Sage Kapila and greeted him with great humility.

Kapila blessed him and said, 'I wish your father and uncles had been as polite as you, my son! You can take back the horse.

I have no idea how it came to be tied here. However, you can tell your grandfather that there is only one way for his sons to be absolved of their sins. The holy goddess Ganga must descend to the earth and bathe their ashes in her waters.

Puzzled and confused, Anshuman returned to Ayodhya.

Ganga had been born when Lord Vishnu, in his Vaman incarnation, pierced the shell of the universe with his toenail. The purest waters flowed through the shell, entered our universe and took the form of a river. This was Ganga. But she remained in the heavens because she was too pure for the sinful earth.

How would Ganga come down to the earth and free the souls of King Sagar's sons? The king prayed, Anshuman prayed but Ganga remained in heaven.

Many, many years passed this way. After Sagar and Anshuman, each descendant of Sagar continued to offer prayers to all the gods.

Finally, the king's great-great-grandson, Bhagirath, was able to please the goddess Ganga with his devotion and piety. However, when he begged her to come to the earth, Ganga told Bhagirath that it was not possible. Her waters flowed with extraordinary power. If she descended from the heavens, the force of their current could destroy the earth.

'Holy mother, there has to be a way!' Bhagirath pleaded. 'I cannot let my ancestors remain cursed forever.'

'Your dedication touches me deeply, my son,' replied the goddess. 'If someone could lessen the force by interrupting the flow, I will happily come down to the earth.'

'I know who can do it,' Bhagirath leapt up excitedly. 'There is only one person. The great Lord Shiva. He has the power to break the fall of your waters.'

'Go to him with my blessings,' Ganga said softly.

Bhagirath set off to find Lord Shiva at Mount Kailash. He fell at his feet with folded hands.

'Great lord,' he pleaded, 'you are the only one who can free the souls of my ancestors. You know what Sage Kapila said—that the waters of the Ganga can wash away their sins. The goddess has agreed but is worried that the force of her waters might destroy the earth. If someone can soften the impact, she will come down.'

'Son, I know that your family has been praying for this miracle for many, many years,' Shiva said.

'It is time to save the souls of your ancestors. I will catch the descending river in my matted locks and soften the force of her flow.'

When Ganga heard that Shiva had agreed, she came rushing down from the heavens like a great storm. Lord Shiva immediately captured the foaming, tumbling waters in his hair and let her stream through the Himalayas. The waiting Bhagirath led her down to the plains at Haridwar, then to her meeting place with the Yamuna at Prayag. Her speed was much reduced by now.

She flowed on to Varanasi, and wound her way to the sea where she entered the Bay of Bengal at the spot we now know as Gangasagar.

When her waters reached the netherworld and touched the ashes of the 60,000 sons of King Sagar, they were delivered from their curse and finally received salvation. Because Bhagirath was the man who brought Ganga to the earth, she is also known as Bhagirathi. And people still believe that bathing in her waters will deliver them from their sins.

Indra and the Ants

Indra defeated Vritra but he felt guilty that he had killed a Brahmin. Vritra, though an asura, was the son of Tvashta, and thus a Brahmin. The gods consoled Indra by saying that he had saved the universe from destruction. They even said that Indra should be crowned once more as king of heaven to celebrate his victory.

A grand coronation ceremony was held and Indra was happy again. In fact, all the praise went to his head and he became quite proud. As the king of heaven, he began to feel he should have a bigger palace now.

He sent for Vishwakarma, the architect of the gods. 'O divine builder,' he said, 'you know what a great victory I have won.'

Vishwakarma nodded. 'Indeed, O king of the devas, you have performed an extraordinary feat. All are singing your praises, both gods and mortals.'

Indra beamed with satisfaction. 'There is only one problem,' he continued. 'My old palace is too small. It's become a bit shabby too. It is not grand enough to suit my position as the newly victorious king of the gods. Please start making plans for a beautiful new palace right away.

Vishwakarma immediately began work on a plan. Once he had completed it, he showed it to Indra.

'It seems alright,' said the king of the gods. 'But remember, the new palace will symbolise my position. It has to be more magnificent than any other building ever constructed.

'Whoever sets eyes on it must be dazzled by its grandeur. They must know at once that the lord of the universe dwells here.'

Vishwakarma began to build a magnificent palace right away. It was a huge structure with polished marble floors that shone like mirrors. Hundreds of marble pillars set with precious jewels held up the carved ceiling. Indra's hall of audience was so large that any ordinary mortal would faint with exhaustion walking from one end to another. Only the gods with their divine powers could cross it easily. Its high-domed roof was covered with gold and gleamed like a diamond in the sun. Indeed, anyone who saw Indra's new palace would be dazzled.

Outside, fountains shot up huge jets of perfumed water. And at the sound of a mantra, beautiful music could be heard. There were tastefully designed gardens with all colourful flowers found in heaven or earth growing in them.

Delighted with his own work, Vishwakarma went to Indra.

'Lord Indra, I have done it! I have built the most magnificent palace that ever existed in this universe,' he cried in excitement. 'Please come and see it.'

Indra flew there immediately in his chariot. But when he started his tour of the new palace, he began to frown. His frown grew deeper and deeper as he looked at all the airy rooms and hallways. He began to point out faults.

'The hall of audience is not impressive enough,' he said. 'My bedroom doesn't have a good view. The carvings on the doors are not fine enough.'

Poor Vishwakarma! He didn't know what to say. 'Lord of the heavens, I have put heart and soul into creating this building!' he cried. 'There is none other like it in the three worlds!'

But Indra simply shook his head. 'It's not grand enough for me. Rebuild it,' he said.

Vishwakarma had no choice but to build another palace. He used all his imagination to design an even more magnificent building. He made it much larger and grander. But once again Indra was not satisfied.

'I'm sorry, Vishwakarma,' he said, waving his hand. 'It's slightly better, but still not good enough for me, the lord of the universe.'

Vishwakarma was in despair but he tried again. He put in all his effort to construct the most splendid palace anyone could dream of. But once again he failed to please Indra.

'You simply have to rebuild it,' Indra said airily. 'Not good enough.'

The divine architect Vishwakarma was exhausted now. He hurried to Brahma for help. 'Do something, Lord Brahma!' he begged. 'This can go on till the end of time. I'm afraid Indra will never be satisfied.'

'Don't worry, Vishwakarma,' Brahma said. 'I'll take care of this problem.'

He went to meet Vishnu and Shiva. After they had exchanged greetings, Brahma said, 'Indra's victory over Vritra has gone to his head. We have to make him see sense or all of us will suffer.'

Together the trinity made a plan.

Indra was standing inside the hall of his new palace and gazing around with a look of dissatisfaction. Suddenly a dark-skinned Brahmin boy entered.

'What a magnificent palace!' he exclaimed.

'Magnificent?' Indra wrinkled his nose. 'You call this magnificent?'

'It is the largest and most splendid palace any Indra has built so far,' said the boy.

'Any Indra? What are you talking about?' Indra asked, amused that a young boy should claim to know about such things.

'Exactly what I said,' insisted the boy. 'To this date, no other Indra has built such a grand palace.'

'Wait a minute,' said Indra. 'I am Indra, the king of the gods. How can you talk about other Indras while I stand here?'

'Don't you know about them?' the boy sounded surprised. 'There have been so many Indras before you. Whenever Brahma falls asleep, the universe is destroyed, along with everything on it. Gods, mortals, everyone and everything. Then when Brahma wakes up again, he creates another universe and a new Indra to rule over it.'

Indra paled. 'How can it be?' he frowned.

He paled further when the boy began to tell him about Indra's ancestors, about the great cycles of creation and destruction.

He even told him about the countless number of worlds scattered through space, each with its own Indra. 'I have seen them all,' he added.

While he was speaking, a procession of ants began to crawl into the hall. The boy looked at the ants and laughed. Indra got very nervous now.

'Why are you laughing?' he asked the boy.

'Because these ants are all former Indras,' the boy replied.

Stunned, Indra could only stare at the ants. Just then, a hermit entered the hall. There was a circular cluster of hair on his chest, with a bare spot in the middle.

Indra was quite puzzled to see the strange-looking hermit. 'Holy one, why is there a bare spot in the middle of your chest?' he asked.

'Each of these hairs represents the life of one Indra,' said the hermit, smiling. 'Each time a hair falls, an Indra dies and another replaces him.'

All of Indra's pride at his achievements vanished immediately.

The Brahmin boy and the hermit were actually Lord Vishnu and Lord Shiva in disguise.

He sent for Vishwakarma and rewarded him for his work, saying he was satisfied now. Then he decided to abandon the pomp of kingship to become a hermit. He would meditate, seek wisdom and do penance for the sin of killing Vritra.

After many years of prayer and meditation, Indra learned how to maintain a balance in his life and returned to his throne.

The Birth of Durga

Rambha, the king of the asuras, took a liking to a lady buffalo and decided to marry her. After sometime, a son was born to them.

He was named Mahishasur, since Mahisha means buffalo and he was the son of a buffalo and an asura. As an asura or demon, he was born with superhuman powers. At that time the devas or gods and the asuras were bitter enemies.

They were always fighting with each other and it was the gods who usually won.

When Mahishasur grew older, he didn't like this one bit. 'Father, why do we always lose to the gods? They have begun to think they are too great,' he would say to Rambha. 'We have to change this around. If only I could grow so strong that even these snooty gods couldn't touch me. If only I could become the most powerful being in all creation!'

'You have my blessings, son,' said his father. 'Maybe one day you shall.'

And so, day and night, all that Mahishasur could think of was about how to become more powerful than the gods.

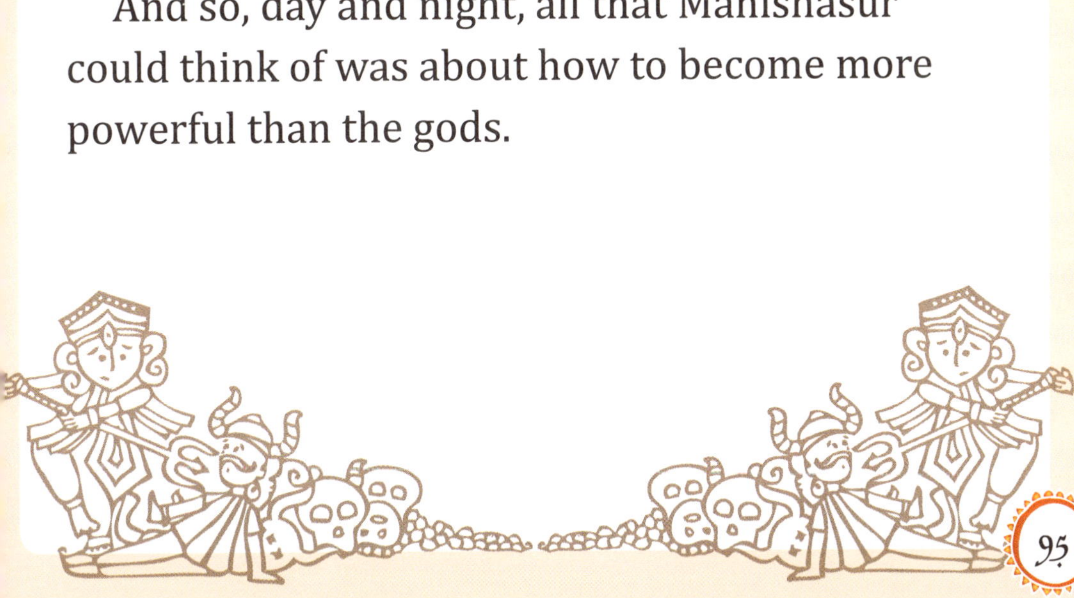

Finally he got an idea.

'Tapasya!' he cried. 'Why didn't I think of it earlier? Everyone knows that strict fasting and prayer can make a person very strong.'

Mahishasur immediately began a long penance. He stopped eating and began to pray to Brahma, the creator, standing on one foot under a tree. Many years passed and Mahishasur continued to stand there, praying. And the longer he stood, the more strength he gained. Soon the time came when the power he had built up through his penance spread through all the three worlds. Even Brahma the creator felt its presence.

'Mahishasur has been praying to me with great devotion for such a long time,' Brahma said to himself. 'He deserves to be rewarded.'

He set off for the place where the asura was fasting. Mahishasur sensed his presence and opened his eyes. When he saw Brahma standing there, he fell at his feet and cried, 'Lord, you have honoured me greatly by coming here. It means you have recognised my devotion and answered my prayers.'

Brahma raised his hand in blessing. 'I am, indeed, very impressed by your long and devoted tapasya. You have fasted for years and prayed to me. I want to grant you a boon. Ask for anything that you desire.'

Mahishasur's heart leapt with joy. 'Lord, I thank you for your kindness,' he replied at once. 'All I ask is that I should become immortal.'

Brahma smiled and shook his head. 'My son, what you ask for is not possible,' he said gently. 'Every creature that is born has to die. Think of something else. I will be happy to grant you a boon.'

Mahishasur was disappointed at first, but he thought quickly. 'There has to be a way,' he said to himself. 'Maybe I can ask for a boon that will make me as good as immortal.' After sometime, he asked Brahma, 'Lord, if you cannot make me immortal, can you grant me the boon that I cannot be killed by either a man or a god? If I have to die, it should only be at the hands of a woman.'

Being a gigantic demon, he was confident that no woman would be strong enough to kill him.

'It shall be as you ask,' Brahma said. 'You will meet your death only at the hands of a woman.'

Mahishasur folded his hands and bowed low before Brahma. 'I thank you for this great boon, Lord,' he said.

The moment Brahma departed, Mahishasur bellowed with triumph and waved his trident in the air. 'Now I will show these weakling gods who the true ruler of the three worlds is!' he yelled. 'No one can harm even a hair on my head, ha-ha!'

His terrible laughter rang through the earth. And Mahishasur lost no time in unleashing a reign of terror. He gathered a huge army of fellow asuras and began to torment the inhabitants of the earth. They beat up travellers and robbed them of their belongings.

They broke into people's houses and took what they wanted. If people fought back or tried to stop them, they killed them without a second thought. Soon, all the inhabitants of the earth were living in fear of the demons.

The news spread everywhere that Mahishasur was invincible and no one could harm him.

After suppressing all the mortals, Mahishasur decided to challenge the gods. He called all his generals for a meeting. 'The gods have always tried to keep us down,' he thundered. 'But it's a different story now. I have Brahma's boon. No man or god can harm me.'

'Get ready for a battle, friends. Tomorrow we will attack Amravati, Indra's capital,' he bellowed.

True to his command, the army of asuras stormed Amravati, confident that they would win. The gods had heard about the coming attack and were quite worried. They consulted Brahma.

'There is little I can do,' he said gravely. 'I was the one who granted the boon of invincibility to Mahishasur. If only I had guessed his intentions!' All the same, he came to the battlefield along with Vishnu and Shiva.

Mahishasur had taken the form of a huge buffalo and was leading the demons.

And to their horror, all the divine weapons of the gods proved useless before his strength. Vishnu hit him with his powerful mace. The demon was stunned but rose again, taking the form of a lion. Then Vishnu threw his chakra to cut off his head but it bounced back, unable to make even a slight cut on him. In revenge, Mahishasur butted the god and knocked Vishnu down.

As a last resort, Indra hurled his thunderbolt vajra at the demon. But he was shocked to see that Mahishasur still stood there, laughing! Indra's mighty thunderbolt passed over him like a gentle breeze. Mahishasur now took the form of a giant buffalo again and redoubled his attack.

The gods began to flee in despair now.

With shouts and whoops of delight, the asura army drove the gods out of heaven. They occupied Indra's palace and poured into the streets of Amravati, singing their frightful songs of victory.

'Now I am lord of the three worlds!' Mahishasur yelled as he sat down on Indra's throne.

There was no one left to check Mahishasur's oppression now. He did what he wanted and the people of the earth suffered terribly.

The gods were in a pathetic state. For years they wandered over fields and mountains.

Then, tired of being in exile, they decided to consult the trinity, Shiva, Vishnu and Brahma to come up with a way to destroy the demon so they could return to heaven.

Vishnu said, 'Not a single woman living in all three worlds is strong enough to destroy this evil creature. Let us use our combined powers to create one.'

The desperate gods closed their eyes and began to concentrate all their thoughts on creating this invincible woman. Their divine powers and deep concentration worked, and soon a fiery pillar of light appeared in the sky. It was so bright that even the gods found it impossible to look at it. It was a mass of pure energy produced from their combined power.

From it they created a goddess who would be strong enough to vanquish Mahishasur.

Shiva created her face, Vishnu gave her arms, and Brahma provided her with legs. The god of the oceans of milk gave her a red sari and a diamond necklace.

Vishwakarma presented her with earrings, bracelets and other jewellery he had made himself. Thus all the gods presented her with various ornaments.

Once she was beautifully dressed, Vishnu said, 'Let us arm her with our special strengths along with invincible weapons.' He began by handing her a chakra like his own. Shiva gave her a trident and Brahma a kamandal full of the holy Ganga water.

Varun gave her a gift of ever-blooming lotus flowers and a mighty conch. Agni presented

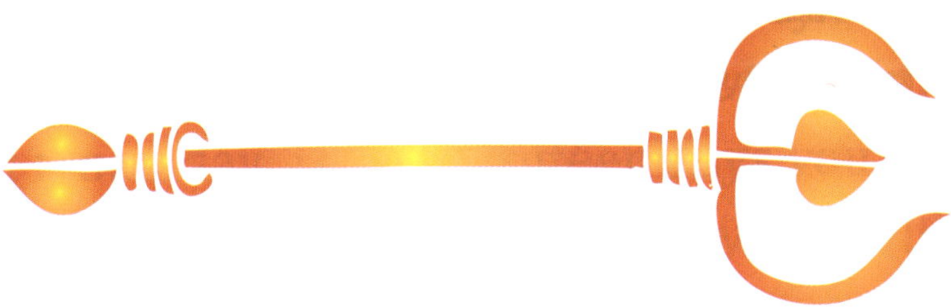

her with the sadagni—a weapon that could kill thousands. Vayu provided her with a bow and a quiver holding an endless supply of arrows. Indra gave her a thunderbolt similar to his own. Vishwakarma armed her with an axe, Yama with a staff and Kuber gave her a cup of wine. Surya presented her with his blinding rays. Tvashta gave her the kaumodoki, the divine mace.

In this way, all the gods gifted her different weapons.

Finally, Himalaya, the god of the mountains, gave her a tiger to ride on and she was named Mahadevi or Durga.

With their blessings, Durga mounted the tiger and set out to destroy Mahishasur.

As she approached Amravati, she let out a mighty roar that shook the mountains and created huge waves in the seas. Mahishasur asked his soldiers to find out what was happening.

When he heard that a woman was challenging him, he laughed and said, 'Tell her that I will be happy to marry her.'

When his messengers brought the proposal, the goddess replied, 'Tell your king that I am no ordinary woman who would be eager to marry him. I am Mahadevi and my husband is Mahadeva. I have come to ask him to leave Amravati and return to his place below the world. If he doesn't go, I will destroy him!'

When he heard this reply, Mahishasur flew into a rage. His leading warriors said arrogantly, 'Your Majesty, we will go and set this silly woman right. She is not worth your attention.'

The asuras went out to fight with Mahadevi. To their astonishment and horror, one after the other the boastful warriors were finished off.

The demon king got the news and became even more furious. 'Cowards and weaklings! They could not stand up to a mere woman. I will settle this wretched female once and for all!' he thundered.

Cunningly, he assumed the form of a handsome man to woo Mahadevi.

'Lovely lady, why do you want to fight like a rough man? Why not marry me, the king of heaven?' he said in the sweetest tones possible. 'Throw these weapons aside and come and live like a queen.'

When she rejected him firmly, Mahishasur attacked the goddess along with an army of asuras. But Durga immediately created a huge troop of soldiers from her breath to fight back. Mahishasur tried all the tricks he knew. He kept changing shape to confuse the goddess. From a man he became a lion, then an elephant. But each time, Mahadevi wounded him severely with her weapons.

The battle raged for nine days. Finally the goddess killed the asura, who had taken the form of a huge buffalo again. She beheaded him with the chakra which Vishnu had given her.

Thus she freed the world from Mahishasur's tyranny. Indra and the other gods returned to the heavens again, and all was well. Since then, Durga is worshipped during the Navratras and is addressed as Mahishasur Mardini.

When Krishna Saved Vrindavan

Govardhan Hill stood tall and proud in the lush green region of Vrindavan. Krishna and his brother Balaram loved to run up and down its slopes with their friends. They would climb trees, play hide and seek in its caves and splash about in the ponds. They also took their cows to graze on the tender, sweet grass that covered the hillsides. When the rainy season arrived, Govardhan Hill became even more beautiful, with different types of herbs and blooming flowers spreading their scent in the air.

It was a pleasant morning during the monsoon season. Krishna woke up to hear the sounds of people chattering happily and singing songs in praise of the rain god Indra. When he peeped out of the door, he saw them decorating the paths with flower garlands and lamps. He watched them hurrying to and fro, dressed in their best, carrying baskets of sweets and fruit, pails of milk and pots of curd.

His father Nand was busy along with the others. When he saw his young son watching curiously, Nand said, 'Come along, Krishna, come and help us.'

But Krishna asked, '*Pitashree*, what is going on? Why have the people left all their work aside to decorate the village? Is there some celebration today?'

'It is time for the annual puja for Lord Indra,' replied his father. 'The people of our village are making arrangements for a grand ceremony. They are gathering all the items they need so that the ritual can be performed in the best way possible. That will please Indra.'

'But why do they have to do it?' Krishna asked.

'My son,' said his father, stroking his head lovingly, 'in Vrindavan, we are all farmers or cowherds. We need rain so that our crops grow well and there is plenty of grass and fodder for the animals to feed. The rains have been good this year and the crops and the grass are growing well. If these prayers and offerings please the rain god, he will be kind to us and continue to send plenty of rain.'

'I don't think that is right!' Krishna cried. 'It's not Indra but Govardhan Hill that brings us good rainfall. When the moist air rises up to the top of the hill, it turns into rain.

'Govardhan Hill also provides us with fresh grass which makes our cows give the best milk. And then, all the villagers work so hard tending to the cattle and taking care of their fields. Isn't that enough to make the god happy? They should not perform this useless ceremony.'

Krishna's remarks caught the attention of some of the villagers. When they noticed that his father Nand was looking thoughtful, they gathered around.

'What is it, Krishna?' asked the village headman. 'Is something bothering you?'

'Yes, uncle,' Krishna said in an urgent tone. 'You get up early in the morning and break your backs to dig the earth and make it ready for planting seeds.

'You toil in the hot sun to weed and manure your crops. You sweat and slog to raise a harvest. We also walk far to find the best grass for our cattle. Now on top of this you have to put in more effort to make the rain god happy. Why do you need to do this? Your hard work should be enough to please Lord Indra. He should bless you for your toil. And actually it is Govardhan Hill that gives us rain. We should worship the mountain instead of Indra.'

The people's eyes opened wide. They looked at each other as if they had made a new discovery.

'Krishna is right,' said an old woman. 'It is Govardhan who gives us many blessings.

'And if he is a kind god, Lord Indra should see how hard we work and send us rain as a reward.'

'Truly spoken,' said a man. 'Let us forget the rituals and go back to our fields.'

Thus the people of Vrindavan did not perform the usual rituals to please the rain god.

Indra was watching from the heaven above, waiting for the annual ceremonies in his praise. When he heard all this, he became furious. 'They are listening to a little boy's silly talk and ignoring me—the great king of the gods, the one who has brought the life-giving gift of rain to them. I will teach these arrogant people of Vrindavan a lesson,' he shouted.

'I will give them such a punishment that they will never forget that I am a god to be feared.'

Indra flung his deadly thunderbolt into the sky. He sent for his most fearsome clouds. 'Go with all your speed to Vrindavan,' he commanded. 'Give them a taste of my power in a manner they will never forget!'

Within minutes, thousands of clouds darkened the sky over Vrindavan. The sun was completely blotted out.

And then rain began to pour down. It rained and rained. It kept raining for seven days and seven nights without stop. The thunder rolled with a terrifying sound and lightning flashed threateningly. The frightened people rushed for shelter. But there was no shelter because the rain poured down with such awful force that people's huts began to be washed away.

Worse, the rivers rose and the whole region became like the sea. The helpless people didn't know what to do. Their cattle were also bellowing with fear and dashing about in panic.

‘What will we do? Where should we go?’ was the cry heard from everywhere as the drenched people tried to save themselves.

Then someone cried, ‘It’s all Krishna’s fault!’

Immediately, others voiced their opinions. ‘Yes,’ they said, ‘if he hadn’t persuaded us to stop the puja for Indra, none of this would have happened.’

‘This is Indra’s punishment for us!’ wailed another. ‘This downpour will drown Vrindavan completely.’

The angry people ran to Krishna. ‘See, you have brought this great calamity upon us,’ they shouted. ‘Now we are going to lose everything, even our lives.

'All because we were foolish enough to listen to you. We ignored the mighty Lord Indra and brought his wrath upon us.'

'What is going to happen now, son?' Nand too cried out in despair.

Krishna held up his hand. 'Let us all try to remain calm,' he said. 'I agree that I told you to stop the ceremony and Indra is angry now. But do not worry. I will save you from this disaster.'

'How will you save us?' yelled a man. 'Can you stop the rain and dry up the floods?'

And then his mouth fell open!

Krishna had lifted the enormous Govardhan Hill on his palm! He was holding it up high like a huge umbrella. 'Come, friends,' he said. 'Come and take shelter under the mountain. Bring all your animals too.'

For a moment the people of Vrindavan were too awestruck to react. Then they quickly herded their frightened animals and hurried to take refuge under the mighty mountain. By now Krishna was balancing it effortlessly on his little finger.

Indra watched from above, dumbstruck with astonishment. 'How did this little cowherd manage such a feat?' he frowned.

'Indra, don't you know that he is not a mere cowherd but the incarnation of Vishnu?' Brahma asked gently.

All the gods gazed at the young boy who was holding up an enormous mountain on his little finger. They began to shower their blessings on him.

Indra felt very ashamed. He withdrew his clouds and bowed to Krishna. After that he did not trouble the people of Vrindavan any longer.

The grateful people fell at Krishna's feet and sang his praises.

Since then Govardhan Puja is celebrated the day after Diwali, to remember how Krishna saved his people from Indra's fury.

How Parvati Won Shiva

The gods were extremely worried. A powerful demon named Tarakasur was terrorising the mortals. Worse, he had even dared to attack the gods. When they found themselves unable to defeat him, Indra and the other gods approached Lord Brahma.

'Help us, O creator!' they pleaded. 'How can we get rid of this demon?'

Brahma thought for a while, then said, 'There is only one being strong enough to defeat Tarakasur. A son of Shiva.'

The gods exchanged troubled glances. 'But Shiva has renounced the world and is meditating in the Himalayas,' they said.

Shiva's beloved wife Sati had burned herself to death in the sacrificial fire after her father Daksha had insulted her husband. Overcome with sorrow, Shiva had gone to the mountains to pray and meditate.

'Go and pray to the goddess Mahadevi,' Brahma said. 'She will tell you a way.'

The gods worshipped Mahadevi with great devotion. Pleased, the goddess said, 'I will take an incarnation and marry Shiva so that this evil demon can be destroyed.'

Soon after, Himavat, the king of the mountains, and his wife, Maina Devi, had a baby daughter. They named her Parvati or "daughter of the mountains". Little did they know that she was Mahadevi in the form of a human.

Parvati was a beautiful girl. She was also kind and good- natured. Right from the beginning she was very devoted to Shiva and would pray to him often.

When she became old enough to get married, many young men came to ask for her hand. However, Parvati refused each one of them. Concerned, her father asked her one day, ‘Dear child, why do you refuse each and every man who asks to marry you?’

‘Father, if I have to marry, there is only one man for me. And that is

Lord Shiva,' Parvati replied in a firm voice.

Himavat and Maina Devi exchanged troubled glances. They knew that Shiva had renounced the world and was performing a severe penance in the Himalayas. How could they make him agree to marry Parvati?

Fortunately, one day the sage Narad happened to pass by their place.

When he heard about their problem, Narad said, 'Take her to Lord Shiva. It will not be easy to persuade him, but for the good of the three worlds it is important that she get married to him. If he refuses to look at her, say she will help him in his worship.'

King Himavat and Queen Maina Devi set off in search of Shiva, along with Parvati.

Finally, they found the god on the Himalayas, deep in meditation. The three of them waited patiently for Shiva to open his eyes. And at last he did.

'What brings you here, O king?' he asked Himavat, not even noticing Parvati who was gazing at him with adoring eyes.

'Lord Shiva, my daughter Parvati has long been your devotee. Now she wishes to assist you in your worship,' Himavat said with folded hands.

'She can, if she wishes to,' said Shiva carelessly. 'She will have to stay here.'

'Thank you, Lord, for granting her this privilege,' Himavat replied.

'My child, serve Lord Shiva as best as you can.'

He and Maina Devi said goodbye to their daughter with tearful eyes. They were not sure if they were doing the right thing, but Parvati was determined. And Narad had also advised them that this was the right thing to do.

Parvati began to live on the bare hillside. She would gather fresh flowers for Shiva's worship, hoping that one day he would reward her devotion. But Shiva remained deep in meditation most of the time. He did not spare a single glance for the lovely girl who would sit there gazing at him for hours.

The gods had felt relieved when Parvati had begun to help Shiva with his worship.

But when they noticed that he remained unmoved, they became worried. Tarakasur was getting completely out of control, harassing innocent and helpless people more and more, and threatening the gods too.

They decided to take matters into their own hands and approached Kamadev, the god of love. 'Please shoot an arrow of love into Shiva's heart,' they said. 'It's the only way to save the universe from destruction.'

'Lord Shiva is deep in meditation,' Kamadev replied. 'He will be furious if I disturb him.'

'You will have to risk his anger to save the world,' said Indra.

Kamadev went to Shiva then, even though his wife Rati advised him not to do it.

Shiva sat there,

eyes tightly closed. Kamadev quickly pulled at his bowstring and let an arrow fly. Sure enough, it pierced Shiva's heart and he opened his eyes. Parvati was the first person he saw. He was charmed by her, but he could not help feel uneasy.

And then Shiva caught sight of Kamadev armed with his famous bow. Furious, he opened his third eye and burned the god of love to ashes.

Parvati had been waiting with a garland in her hands to offer it to him. But Shiva closed his eyes again and returned to his meditation.

The gods were horrified and wondered what was to be done. Little did they know how determined Parvati was!

Her parents hurried there when they heard what had happened. 'He has insulted you!'

Himavat cried. 'Forget him. There are other men far more worthy of you.'

'No, father, I cannot give up so easily,' Parvati said. 'I too will undertake a penance and show him that I'm as determined as him.'

Parvati began to pray and meditate too. She lived only on wet leaves, hoping that her severe penance would have some effect on Shiva. Years went by but Shiva did not open his eyes. Then Parvati began a harsher penance, eating only dry leaves.

When it did not have any effect on the god, she gave up eating leaves altogether and became known as Aparna, which means "one who does not eat even a leaf".

During the course of her meditation she gained the knowledge that she was an incarnation of Mahadevi and had been Sati, Shiva's wife in a previous birth. This made her even more determined. The news of her resolute tapasya spread far and wide and many sages and holy men came to pay their respects to her.

Only Shiva remained unmoved. Finally Parvati stopped drinking water, and began living on nothing but air.

The power of Parvati's penance began to affect her surroundings. It created heat in the atmosphere. Soon the gods felt it too and rushed to Brahma and Vishnu again.

'What is to be done?' they cried. 'Shiva must relent or the whole universe will catch fire from the heat of Parvati's penance.'

Brahma and Vishnu hurried to Shiva. 'Lord Shiva, the whole universe is at risk,' they said. 'Only you can save creation. Please answer Parvati's prayers.'

When they explained, Shiva understood their point. But he wanted to test Parvati's devotion some more.

The next morning, Parvati was ready to begin her prayers when a handsome young man approached her.

'They say you are performing a tapasya to marry Shiva,' the man said. 'I'm very surprised that a beautiful girl like you can even think of someone like Shiva. He is such a rough fellow. Do you really want a husband who smears ash on himself, wears a necklace of skulls and likes to live in cremation grounds? You would be better off if you marry a normal man like me.'

'What do you know about Shiva?' Parvati asked angrily. 'He is the master of the three worlds and the only man I love. I will continue my penance till he recognises my devotion. Kindly leave this place at once.'

Parvati was turning away in a rage when a flash of light dazzled her.

Shiva had assumed his true form!

'I am touched by your deep devotion, Parvati,' he said. 'I want to grant you a boon. Please ask for anything you desire.'

Parvati was speechless with joy and astonishment. However, she recovered quickly. 'Lord,' she said with folded hands, 'I cannot tell you how grateful I am that you answered my call. There is only one boon I desire and that is to marry you.'

'Granted!' Shiva said immediately. That was exactly what he too wanted now. He had recognised that she was his beloved Sati who had come back to him in a new incarnation.

Shiva and Parvati got married and everyone rejoiced. After some time Parvati gave birth to a son whom they named Kartikeya. When he grew older, Kartikeya killed Tarakasur and all was well again.

Parvati and Shiva are considered the ideal couple among the gods. And to this day, women worship Parvati to be blessed with a happy married life.

Author, poet and translator, Deepa Agarwal writes for both children and adults and has over 50 books published. A frequent contributor to magazines and journals in India and abroad, she has edited and compiled several anthologies. Among various other awards, she received the N.C.E.R.T. National Award for Children's Literature in 1993 for her picture book *Ashok's New Friends*, while her historical fiction *Caravan to Tibet* was on the IBBY (International Board on Books for Young People) Honour List 2008. Five of her books have been included in the White Raven catalogue of the International Youth Library Munich. Recent titles include *The Wish-fulfilling Cow and Other Classic Indian Tales* (Scholastic India) *Listen, O King!* a retelling of the thousand year old Vikram-Vetal stories based on the Sivadasa version in the Puffin Classics series and an edited anthology *Best World Stories* (Red Turtle/Rupa).

Published by Scholastic India Pvt. Ltd.
A subsidiary of Scholastic Inc., New York, 10012 (USA).
Publishers since 1920, with international operations in Canada,
Australia, New Zealand, the United Kingdom, India, and Hong Kong.

For information regarding permission, write to:
Scholastic India Pvt. Ltd.
A-27, Ground Floor, Sigma Centre
Infocity-1, Sector 34, Gurgaon 122001 (India)

First edition: August 2017

ISBN-13: 978-93-5275-175-4

This reprint edition: October 2024, January 2026

Printed in India at Sterling Graphics Pvt. Ltd., Manesar